The Pres and an Officer

HAROLD PINTER

The Pres and an Officer

with a foreword by Antonia Fraser

FABER & FABER

This edition first published in 2018
by Faber and Faber Limited
Bloomsbury House
74–77 Great Russell Street
London WC1B 3DA

First published in the *Guardian*, 28 October 2017

Typeset by Country Setting, Kingsdown, Kent CT14 8ES
Printed and bound in Great Britain
by CPI Group (UK) Ltd, Croydon CR0 4YY

A CIP record for this book is available from the British Library

ISBN 978-0-571-34670-7

2 4 6 8 10 9 7 5 3 1

Foreword

I did something I've never done before. I scribbled some notes on a page from one of Harold's yellow legal pads because I was waiting for a taxi to go to Mass, and too lazy to go upstairs.

I took all the leftover pads when Harold died on Christmas Eve 2008, and for sentimental reasons kept them. Although, up till now, I have never written anything on any of them. But about a month ago, I installed one in a writing case in the drawing room, in theory for occasional use, but really out of tenderness for the past.

When I had written the note, I stripped off the yellow page. Then I nearly fainted. Beneath lay Harold's unforgettable handwriting – although rather frail – and a title: 'The Pres and an Officer'.

Six pages followed, his handwriting getting noticeably stronger. Now the unbelievability of it all increased. Because I could have been reading something written today, written by Harold about Trump. This was a morning when nuclear war, or something like it, appeared to be threatened by Trump on the 8 a.m. news.

Everything was pure Harold, including the cutting of the last line (still visible).

'What would Harold have thought of Trump?' People are always asking me that question. Now we know. As it were.

A.F.

The Pres and an Officer

PRES *ruminating.* OFFICER *reading* Washington Post.

PRES

OK. Get me Strategic Air Command.

OFFICER

Yes. Mr P. Anyone in particular?

PRES

Who do you think?

OFFICER

Well, I –

PRES

The Commander. The Commander.

OFFICER

Yes Sir.

Dials.

OFFICER

Commander? The President of the United States.

PRES

Hi there – who's this? Yes, I know you're the
Commander, but which one? Do I know you?

Voice.

Charley! Of course I know you, Charley. How you doing?

Voice.

Good. Good. And the folks?

Voice.

Great. That's good news. Now hear this. This is a Presidential Command and I want it deployed forthwith. Get me? Nuke London.

Silence. Voice.

That's right. London. That's right. London. Straight away.

Voice.

Congress? Fuck Congress. What are you talking about?

Voice.

What international community? Are you joking? Listen, I've said it once and I'll [say] it just one more time. Nuke London. This is a Presidential Decree.

Voice.

Okay. Good. And let me know how it goes.

Phone down.

Silence.

You know what I'd really like? A double Jack Daniel's on the rocks. But of course I gave up booze for God. The whole world knows that.

OFFICER

You just gave instructions to nuke London.

PRES

You bet. They've had it coming to them for a long time. What do you think?

Rubs his hands.

They've had it coming to them and boy are they going to get it?

OFFICER

But I'm just mildly surprised that it's London.

PRES

Those cheapskates. Those horizontal pricks. Those scumbags. An elephant never forgets. Nor does a President.

OFFICER

But I thought they were on our side.

PRES

Our side! Traitors. Stinkypoos. Can't speak a damn word of English.

OFFICER

They can't speak English? Why not?

PRES

Because they're French, you fool. They live in Froggy land. Well, the Froggy Circus is over. Jesus. I think I'll have a drink. I know God won't mind. He's very fond of me.

OFFICER

London in England.

PRES

What?

OFFICER

London is the capital of England. They are our allies.
Our best friends. Our only friends.

PRES

London? What do you mean?

OFFICER

London is not in France. Paris is in France. Paris is the
capital of France.

PRES

I thought Paris was the capital of England.

OFFICER

France.

PRES

You mean I'm nuking the wrong place?

OFFICER

Afraid. So.

PRES

Call Charley. Tell him I revoke the order.

OFFICER *dials*.

OFFICER

Commander. The Pres says revoke his last order.

Voice.

Thank you. (*To* PRES.) London is being nuked at this very moment.

PRES

But can't somebody explain to them? I just got it wrong, that's all. Don't we have an Embassy over there, in London.

OFFICER

They're all dead. London has gone.

PRES

OK. I'll tell you what I'll do. The bastards. I'll tell you what I'll do. Give me the Commander.

Phone.

Charley? It's the President. How are the folks?

Voice.

Good. Great. That's good news. Now listen. They're not going to get away with this. The bastards. Nuke Paris.

Facsimile of the Manuscript

The exact date of authorship is not known.

*Any changes from the original manuscript
are made with agreement of the Pinter Estate.*

The Pres r an Officer

Pres. ruminating. Officer
reading Washington Post.

P— OK. Get me Strategic Air
Command.

O— Yes. Mr. P. Anyone in
particular?

P— Who do you think?

O— Well, I —

P— The Commander. The Commander.

O— Yes Sir.

Dials

O — Commander? The Pres. of
the US.

P— Hi's there. Who's this?
Yes, I know your the
Commander, but which one!
Do I know you?
                    voice
Charley! Of course I know
you, Charlie. How you
doing?
                voice
Good. Good. And the
folks?

[15]

Voice.

P – Great. That's good news.
Now hear this. This is a
Presidential Command &
I want it deployed forthwith.
Get me? Nuke London.

          Silence. Voice.
That's right. London. That
right. London. Straightaway.
                 Voice.
Congress? Fuck Congress.
What are you talking about?
                 Voice
What International Community?
Are you 'joking' Custer, I've
said it once & I'll it púut
once more. Nuke London.
And This is a Presedential
Decree.
          Voice.
Okay. God. And let me
know how it goes.
          phone down.
          Silence.
You know what I'd really
like? a double Jack Daniels
on the rocks. But of course
I gave up booze for God.
The whole world thoughtful.

[17]

5.

O— You just gave instructions
to nuke London.

P— You bet. They've had it coming
to them for a long time.
What do you think? (rubs
his hands). They've had it
coming to them & boy are
they going to get it!

O— But I'm just mildly
surprised that it's London.

P— Those cheapskates. Those
horizontal pricks. Those
scumbags. An elephant
never forgets. Nor does
a President.

O— But I thought they were on
our side.

P— Our side! Traitors.
Stinkypoos. Can't speak
a damn word of English.

O— They can't speak English?
Why not?

P— Because they're French, you
fool. They live in Froggy
Land. Well, the Froggy
Circus is over. Jesus.
I think I'll have a drink.
I know God won't mind.

[19]

P — He's very fond of me.

    S

O — London is England.

P — What?

O — London is the capital of
    England. They are our allies.
    Our best friends. Our only
    friends.

P — London? What do you mean?

O — London is not in France.
    Paris is in France. Paris
    is the capital of France.

P — I thought Paris was the capital
    of England.

O — France.

P — ~~you~~   S.

P — You mean I'm bombing the
    wrong place?

O — Afraid. So.

P — Call Charley. Tell him I
    revoke the order.
           O dials.

O — Commander. The Pres. says
    revoke his last order.

           V.

    Thank you. (to P) London
    is being bombed at this
    very moment.

[21]

P— But cant somebody explain
to them? I just got it
wrong, thats all. Dont we
have an Embassy over there,
in London

O— Theyre all dead. London has
gone.

P— OK. I'll tell you what i'll do.
The bastards. I'll tell you
what I'll do. Give me the
Commander.

    phone.
Charley? Its the President
How are the forces?

Good. Great. Thats good news.
Now listen. Theyre not.
going to get away with this.
~~The bastards. Nuke Paris.~~